CADMUS AND HERMIONE;
&, PERSEUS

Borgo Press Books by PHILIPPE QUINAULT

Alcestis: A Play in Five Acts
Atys: A Play in Five Acts
Cadmus and Hermione; &, Perseus: Two Plays
Isis: A Play in Five Acts

CADMUS AND HERMIONE; &, PERSEUS

TWO PLAYS

PHILIPPE QUINAULT

Translated and Adapted by Frank J. Morlock

THE BORGO PRESS
MMXII

CADMUS AND HERMIONE; &, PERSEUS

Copyright © 2003, 2006, 2012 by Frank J. Morlock

FIRST EDITION

Published by Wildside Press LLC

www.wildsidebooks.com

DEDICATION

*For my cyber friends,
Buford Norman and Horvalis*

CONTENTS

CADMUS AND HERMIONE: A Play in Five Acts 9
CAST OF CHARACTERS. 11
PROLOGUE: The Serpent Python 15
ACT I 27
ACT II 43
ACT III 57
ACT IV 71
ACT V 81
PERSEUS: A Play in Five Acts. 89
CAST OF CHARACTERS. 91
PROLOGUE 95
ACT I 103
ACT II 117
ACT III 133
ACT IV 141
ACT V 157
ABOUT THE AUTHOR 165

CADMUS AND HERMIONE
A PLAY IN FIVE ACTS

For Buford Norman

CAST OF CHARACTERS

PALES

RUSTIC DIVINITIES

MELISSA

TROUPE OF NYMPHS AND SHEPHERDS

THE GOD PAN

ARCAS, companion of Pan

SERVANTS OF PAN WHO DANCE

SERVANTS OF PAN WHO PLAY THE FLUTE

ENVY

FOUR SUBTERRANEAN WINDS

FOUR WINDS OF THE AIR

SIX DANCING SUBTERRANEAN WINDS

THE SUN

TWO DANCING SHEPHERDS

CADMUS, son of Agenor, King of Tyre and brother of Europa

FIRST TYRIAN PRINCE

SECOND TYRIAN PRINCE

ARBAS, an African in Cadmus' following

TWO OTHER AFRICANS, companions of Arbas

THE PAGE OF CADMUS

HERMIONE, daughter of Mars and Venus

CHARITE, one of the Graces, companion of Hermione

AGLANTA, another companion of Hermione

NURSE OF HERMIONE

THE PAGE OF HERMIONE

DRACO, giant, King of Aonia

FOUR GIANTS, servants of Draco

THE GIANT'S PAGE

JUNO

PALLAS

LOVE

A HIGH PRIEST OF MARS

A DRUMMER

THE GOD MARS

FOUR FURIES

ECHION, one of the combatants of the children of the earth

JUPITER

VENUS

HYMEN

PROLOGUE
THE SERPENT PYTHON

The subject of this prologue is taken from the first book of the eighth fable of the Metamorphoses, in which Ovid describes the birth and death of the monstrous serpent, Python, which the Sun caused to be born from the slimy mud remaining on the earth after the flood, and which became a monster so terrible that Apollo himself was obliged to destroy it. The allegorical sense of this subject is so clear that it is unnecessary to explain it. It suffices to say that the king praised it more than usual, and that to form some idea of the grandeur and splendor of his glory, it was necessary to raise it to divinity of light which is the body of his coat of arms.

The stage represents a countryside, with hamlets revealed on both sides and a swamp in the back; a dazzling dawn is seen, followed by a rising Sun whose shining globe rises on the horizon to the sounds of the music playing the overture. Pales, goddess of shepherds, and Melissa, goddess of forests and mountains, come in from opposite sides of the theatre and call the troupes that are accustomed to follow them.

PALES

Hurry shepherds, run.

MELISSA

The voices of birds are calling us.

PALES

Our fields are lit up.

MELISSA

Our hills are golden.

PALES

Everything is shining with the splendor of new light.

MELISSA

Thousands of flowers are being born around us.

PALES AND MELISSA

May the star that lights us make nature beautiful!
Let's not lose a single moment
Of a day so sweet and charming!

(The chorus repeats these last two verses and continues

to sing.)

CHORUS

Let's admire, admire the star which lights us;
Let's sing the glory of its works.
May all the world revere
The God that makes our fine weather.

(Pan, the god of shepherds, appears accompanied by players of rustic instruments and rustic dancers, who come to take part in the rejoicing of the Nymphs and Shepherds and all together begin to form a sort of fest in celebration of the God who gives daylight.)

PAN

Let each experience
The charming sweetness
That the Sun spreads through these lucky climes.
There's nothing that doesn't enchant
In these abodes full of attractions.
Everything laughs here, everything sings here;
Hey! why aren't we laughing?

(The rustic dancers who followed the god Pan, begin a celebration, which is interrupted by subterranean noises and by a sort of night which darkens the stage entirely, and that suddenly obliges the rustic assembly to flee with shouts of terror that forms a sort of terrifying concert with the subterranean noises.)

CHORUSES

What sudden disorder!
What frightful uproar increases!
What appalling tumult!
What abysses are opening under our feet!
The day pales, the heavens are troubled;
The earth is going to vomit hell in its wrath
Let's flee, flee; save ourselves, escape!

(In this sudden darkness, Envy comes out of its cave which opens in the midst of the stage; it evokes the monstrous serpent Python which appears in the slimy swamp, casting fire from its jaws and eyes, which are the only light illuminating the theatre; it calls the most impetuous winds to second its fury; it releases four of those which are locked in subterranean caverns and causes four others to descend which form storms, all of which, after having flown and crossed each other in the air, come to range around it to help it disturb the beautiful weather the Sun had given to earth.)

ENVY

It's too much to see the Sun shine in its career;
The rays which it hurls everywhere
Extremely wound my eyes.
Come, dark enemies of its lively light,
Join our furious distractions.
Let each second me
Appear, frightful monsters,

Arise, subterranean winds, with others more strong;
Fly, tyrants of the air, disturb the earth and the ocean.
Spread terror,
Let heaven roar with us,
Let hell answer us.
Let's fill the earth with horror,
So that nature is confounded.
Let's throw into all the world's hearts
The jealous fury
Which tears apart my heart.

(Envy distributes serpents to the winds which form vortexes around her.)

ENVY

(continuing to sing) And you, monster, arm yourself to injure

This powerful star that knew how to produce you.
He spreads too many blessings, he receives too many prayers.
Agitate your slimy swamp.
Excite a thousand mortal vapors against him.
Deploy, spread your wings,
Let all the impetuous winds
Strive to extinguish his fires.

(The winds form new vortexes, as the serpent Python rises in the air and flies around in circles.)

ENVY

Let's all dare to obscure his most beautiful illumination.
Let us dare to oppose ourselves to his too fortunate career.
What features have broken through the cloud?
What flaming torrent is opening a brilliant passage?
Sun, you triumph, all give way to your power.
How many honors you are going to receive?
Ah! what rage! ah! what rage!
What despair! what despair!

(Flaming darts pierce the thickness of the clouds and dissolve on the serpent Python, which after struggling for some time in the air, falls burnt into its slimy swamp; a rain of fire spreads over the entire stage and forces Envy to sink with its four subterranean winds, while the winds of the air steal away and at the same moment the clouds dissipate and the stage becomes entirely light. The rustic assembly which terror had driven away returns to celebrate the victory of the Sun and to prepare triumphs and sacrifices.)

PALES

Let's drive off fear that troubles us.

MELISSA

Nothing ought to frighten us any more.

PAN

The monster is dead, the storm ceases,
The sun is victor.

PALES

Let superb altars

Be prepared for him.

MELISSA

Let them be adorned
With immortal ornaments.

CHORUS

Let's protect the memory
Of his victory
With a thousand diverse honors.
Let's spread the report of his glory
To the end of the universe.

PALES

But the Sun is advancing,
He's disclosing himself to the eyes of all.

CHORUS

Let's respect his presence

With a profound silence.
Let's listen, let's be silent.

THE SUN

(in his chariot)

It's not through the dazzle of a pompous sacrifice
That I am pleased to see my cares rewarded.
For the reward of my labors, it is enough for me
That each joys in them.
I make the sweetest of my wishes
That of making the whole world happy.
In these fortunate climes, the Muses are going to descend.
Gallant games will follow on their heels.
I inspire songs full of allures
That you are going to hear.
While I am pursuing my career
Profit by the good weather.

(The Sun rises in the heavens, and all the rustic assembly form games in which songs are mixed with dances.)

CHORUS

Let's profit by the good weather.

PALES

Let's all follow the same wish.

CHORUS

Let's profit by the good weather.

MELISSA

Let's love; that's agreeable to all of us.

CHORUS

Let's profit by the good weather

PALES AND MELISSA

The most beautiful days of life
Are ruined without love.

CHORUS

Let's profit by the good weather.

(While the nymphs and rustic gods dance with shepherds and shepherdesses, Pales and Melissa and Pan mix their voices with the rustic instruments.)

PALES, MELISSA, AND PAN

Happy who can please!
Lucky lovers!
Their days are charming;
Love knows how to make them
A thousand sweet moments.

What's the use of youth
To hearts without tenderness?
Whoever has no love
Never has a fine day.
Vainly winter passes.
Vainly in the fields
Everything charms our senses;
A soul of ice
Has no Springtime.
It must break
Of a heart too strict.
Whoever has no love
Never has a fine day.

(Arcas, one of the forest gods, sings and all the instruments and all the voices respond to him, while the rustic assembly, dances and rejoices with oak branches, with which it forms several pleasant figures.)

ARCAS

Can one do better,
When one knows how to please,
Can one do better
Than to love well?
Whatever discomfort that love makes
It's still a charming fetter.
Too much repose often tires.
What can one do with a heart that never loves?
Love satisfies,
Its pains enchant.

Love satisfies,
Everything is fine.
In the fine days of our life,
Pleasures are in season
And some little amorous folly
Is often worth more than too much reason.

CURTAIN

ACT I

The action takes place in the country of Greece which was called Aonia, and that of Cadmus named Boeotia.

The stage represents a garden.

FIRST TYRIAN PRINCE

What! Cadmus, son of a king who holds under his power
The fecund shores of the Nile and the hot regions;
Cadmus, after two years spent far from Tyre,
Foreigner, amongst these Greeks, no longer impatient
To see again a country whose hope he is,
And leaves without regret, so many desolated hearts!

THE TWO TYRIAN PRINCES

(together)

We will follow your destiny everywhere without resistance.
Will it always be necessary for us to be exiles?

CADMUS

I would love to see again the climes of my birth.
But before I can taste the sweetness of it,
I have sworn to achieve a just revenge.

FIRST PRINCE

And yet, lord,
You allow your great heart to languish in these parts.

CADMUS

After having wandered over the earth and the ocean,
Without finding my sister Europa;
After having vainly sought her ravisher,
Heaven here is terminating my vagabond life.
And it's to obey the oracles of the gods
That I must stay in these parts.

FIRST PRINCE

If you find it's the gods
Whose order directs you
To choose this abode,
The god that your heart consults more
Perhaps is Love.

SECOND PRINCE

Could it be possible
That an invincible hero

Could have a heart that only
Love would know how to charm?

CADMUS

What heart is not made to love?
And to be a hero, must one be callous?
What's the use of indomitable courage against Hermione?
The god Mars is her father,
She has a noble pride in it.
The mother of Love is her mother.
She beauties in it.

FIRST PRINCE

What's the use of a love that has no hope?
Hermione is in the power
Of a tyrant who reigns in these parts.

CADMUS

He's a frightful giant, he's an odious monster.

SECOND PRINCE

He's of the blood of Mars, that god favors him,
And in the end, he's the one to whom Hermione is promised.
No other mortals may be her spouse,
And if you attempt the fatal enterprise
Heaven will arm itself against you.

CADMUS

Well! I will perish if destiny decrees it;
I intend to deliver Hermione,
And if I undertake it in vain
I won't know a better destiny to perish for.
Where are our Africans? Let their troupe advance.
The princess wants to see their most gallant dance.
Why is it only one of them appears?

ARBAS

(entering)

Your orders are followed, lord, and everything is ready;
But the tyrant has got it in his head
That only his giants will dance at this feast.

CADMUS

How to make those frightful colossuses move?

ARBAS

When they said to him
how? he replied, I wish it.
These great men, full of chimeras,
Are of a troublesome judgment.
And proud of being above ordinary men
Think that reason must be beneath them.
I've not been able to keep in bounds;
I have fumed against him; I've vomited a thousand

insults;
I've called him tyrant a hundred times.

CADMUS

One must always respect kings.

ARBAS

Were he to have strangled me,
I would not have been able to keep silent.
I was too enraged.
If I had said nothing
I would have choked on spite.

CADMUS

Let's satisfy the giant, he is master here;
Hermione is submissive to his cruel power
This diversion, whatever it may be, in the end
Is worth some time to me for the pleasure of seeing her.
If I'm not allowed to speak to her myself
And to dare to say that I love her,
At least our Africans, by means of their sweetest songs,
Will be able to show her my intense love,
Despite a jealous rival.
Let's prepare everything carefully.
Let's hurry, the princess is coming forward.

ARBAS

Let's go.

CADMUS

You, don't follow my steps.
I am going to see the giant, you must avoid him.

ARBAS

No, no, we won't have further uproar nor fuss.
As to the insults I uttered,
I said them so low
That he didn't hear me.

(Exit Cadmus, Arbas and the two Princes. Hermione enters from another direction with her suite, Charite, Aglanta, and her Nurse.)

HERMIONE

This pleasant abode,
So peaceful and so somber,
Offering silence and shade
To whoever wants to avoid uproar and bright daylight.
Ah! It's not as easy
To find an asylum
To avoid Love!
The pitiless tyranny
Whose barbarous rule I follow
Doesn't forbid loving song and harmony.

You who keep me company,
Reply to my voice.

AGLANTA

It's useless to flee Love, one cannot avoid it.
You can only oppose a vain defense against its features;
Might as well really spare oneself the trouble
By surrendering without resistance.

CHARITE

The pain of love is charming;
There isn't any heart that's exempt
From paying this fatal tribute.
If Love terrifies,
It's more from fright than ill.

NURSE

What choice is in your power!
Think to what spouse heaven wants to join you.

HERMIONE

I shiver when I think of it.
Why do you make me recall it?

NURSE

You are without hope on this side of the earth.

The king who detains you in this charming abode,
Has the god of war for him.
He's assembled in his court
The rest of the giants who escaped the thunder.
For Cadmus sake, beware of an unfortunate passion;
The gift of your heart will cost his life.

HERMIONE

Ah! What cruelty to wish to force on me
This odious choice that I cannot endure!

NURSE

The whole world finds you pitiable,
Yet no one dares to help you.

AGLANTA

Here come the Africans; but the giants are following them.

HERMIONE

What! Everywhere giants!
What! Still disturbing us!

CHARITE

It's customary that pleasures arrive;
What an annoying nuisance,
If they are always coming to meddle with them.

(Enter four giants, two Tyrian Princes, the Giant, three Pages, thirteen Africans, dancing and singing with the guitar, Africans playing with the guitar, two other Africans, singing. Also Cadmus and Arbas. One of the Africans plants a large palm in the midst of the stage; this tree is decorated with several festoons and garlands. The four giants mix with the Africans, and together form a dance mixed with singing.)

ARBAS

(singing with two Africans)

Follow, let's follow Love;
Let's allow ourselves to be enflamed.
Ah! ah! ah! How sweet it is to love!

FIRST AFRICAN

When Love directs us
We will endure his rigors;
Cherish his labors;
He exempts no one
From his conquering arrows.
What peril astonishes us!
Let's leave trembling to weak hearts.

ARBAS AND THE TWO AFRICANS

Follow, let's follow Love;
Let's allow ourselves to be inflamed.

Ah! ah! ah! How sweet it is to love!

SECOND AFRICAN

(singing) Two lovers can sham
When they are in agreement;
The more love finds to fear
The greater effort he makes.
Useless to constrain him
He's much stronger.

ARBAS AND THE TWO AFRICANS

Follow, let's follow Love;
Let's allow ourselves to be inflamed.
Ah! ah! ah! How sweet it is to love!

ALL THREE TOGETHER

There's no charming
Easily
And without alarms;
But in love, all pleases.
There's no torment
Without charms.
Follow, let's follow Love,
Let's allow ourselves to be inflamed.
Ah! ah! ah! How sweet it is to love.

(After the entrance, Hermione rises from the place where she was seated near the giant, who follows her and stops her before she can retire.)

GIANT

It's time to end my pain
After so many unjust refusals.
Where do you intend to go?
Are you fleeing, cruel fair?

HERMIONE

I was here for an African dance;
The Africans are no longer dancing.

GIANT

Nothing must thwart me any more.
Mars is on my side; he's your father.
It's he who intends to join your heart and mine.

HERMIONE

I am the sister of Love, and Venus is my mother.
They are not on your side; do you count them as nothing?

GIANT

Your destiny must
Submit to the decree of the god who gave you life.
And marriage
Doesn't take the opinion of Love.

You fear the reasons with which I can confound you;
You don't listen to me! You want to avoid me!

HERMIONE

When one has nothing to reply,
What's the use of listening?

GIANT

I will follow you everywhere despite your wrath
I intend to present myself ceaselessly to your sight.
And if that doesn't please you,
It will do to torment you.

((All leave except Cadmus, the two Tyrian Princes and a page.)

CADMUS

Abandoning her to this cruel torture is too much.
It's time to cry out
And to dare to attempt all
Against so much injustice.

FIRST PRINCE

That exposes your life to horrible risks;
You will have to subdue the frightful dragon of Mars.

SECOND PRINCE

You must sow its teeth and suddenly see the earth
Form soldiers to make war on you.

THE TWO PRINCES TOGETHER

You see to what dangers you are going to offer yourself.

CADMUS

I only see Hermione, and I am seeing her suffer;
All gives way to this extreme horror;
It is less terrible to die
Than to see the one you love suffering.
Nothing can dismay me;
Despite all perils, Love wants me to hope.

JUNO

(entering in her Chariot) Where are you going, bold one?
What course are you rushing on?
It's the spouse and sister of the master of thunder,
The mother of the God of War;
It's Juno who is coming to stop you.

PALLAS

(in her chariot) Go, Cadmus, let nothing astound you.
Go, fear neither Juno nor the God of combats;

Dare to help Hermione;
You see on your side the Warrior, Pallas.
Run the greatest dangers, I will follow your steps;
It's Jupiter who is ordering me.

JUNO

Who would ever have dared to believe it?
Today, Pallas declares for the lovers!

PALLAS

Who can be against Love
When he agrees with Glory?

JUNO

Avoid a dangerous wrath.

PALLAS

Profit by honest advice.

JUNO

Flee a horrifying death.

PALLAS

Seek in perils an immortal glory.

CADMUS

Between two deities who suspend my prayers,
I don't dare to resist one of the two,
But I am following Love, who calls me.

JUNO

I will pursue your life.

PALLAS

I am flying to your succor.

(Juno and Pallas are carried off in their chariots.)

CURTAIN

ACT II

The stage represents a palace.

ARBAS

Charite, it's very true; Cadmus wishes to attempt
To place Hermione in complete liberty;
He said that to the tyrant and I just heard him.

CHARITE

And what did the giant say? Isn't he irritated?

ARBAS

He laughed at his temerity.
My master ought to see the princess
Before attacking the furious dragon
Which watches guard over these parts.
And love, which urges me toward you,
Wants me to come pay my goodbyes.
Seeing you, beautiful Charite,
I thought that love was a charming pleasure;
But when I must leave you,

I endure nothing but a cruel torture;
Sorrow seizes me, I can't talk any more;
When I weep and when I cry,
You laugh and nothing moves your indifferent heart.

CHARITE

You make a face when weeping.
I can't prevent myself from laughing.

ARBAS

Pity, at least, ought to really induce you
To take some share in my intense sorrows.

CHARITE

If it's really true that you love me,
Why do you want to afflict me?

ARBAS

To assuage my heart of the pain which presses it,
Will it cost you so much to be afflicted a little?

CHARITE

It's a poison that saddens it.
Love is not pleasant any more, 'cause it's no longer a
    game.

ARBAS

One consoles a lover for the rigors of absence
By tender goodbyes.

CHARITE

When it's necessary to leave, a little indifference
Consoles even more.

ARBAS

You actually told me that it was impossible
That your barbarous heart would lose it's harshness.

CHARITE

At least, if you are going to
Complain of seeing me insensitive,
You ought to be satisfied with my sincerity;
Since at last, to satisfy you,
I am not able to weep with you;
If you wanted to please me,
You would laugh with me.

ARBAS

It's too much to jest over my martyrdom.
Scorn ought to deliver me.
Isn't it really mad to cry over
Some one who does nothing but laugh?

CHARITE

Cure yourself, if you can.
I approve of your anger.
When one causes
An amorous heart to despair,
It's through a lucky scorn
That it must escape from the affair.

CHARITE AND ARBAS

When one causes
An amorous heart to despair,
It's through a lucky scorn
That it must escape from the affair.

ARBAS

But the nurse is coming, I have to distance myself.

CHARITE

You know that you please her; do you intend to disdain her?
She's a pretty enough conquest.

ARBAS

If I please her, so much the worse for her.

NURSE

(entering) What! As soon as I appear, you flee the same moment!
When you have friends, is this the way to leave them?

ARBAS

Time presses, and Cadmus is waiting for me.

NURSE

When you were speaking alone to Charite,
Time didn't press you so much;
What charm does she have that attracts you?
What do I have that makes you leave?

ARBAS

I had to speak to her,
I have nothing to tell you.
I must follow Cadmus; we are leaving this place.

NURSE

To tell me goodbye is an obligation
That nothing relieves you of.

ARBAS

Then I say goodbye to you.

(Exit Arbas.)

NURSE

He's leaving me, the ingrate!
He's fleeing me, the faithless one!
Don't be afraid I'll call you back
Go, run, I am letting you leave.
Go, I've nothing more for you but mortal hate.
May you meet the most cruel death;
May the dragon swallow you.

CHARITE

Believe me,
Moderate the outburst of your rage.
A scorn that makes so much uproar
Does too much honor to those who flee us.

NURSE

Ah! Truly, I find you good!
Is it for you, little sprout,
To find fault with what I say?
Wait for the age
When you are wise
To give advice.

CHARITE

I am young, I confess it.
Do you find this defect so worthy of scorn?

Has one no good sense except by losing youth?
It would be very dear at that price.

NURSE

Time ripens wits;
Wit's the fruit of age.

CHARITE

It's not certain that wisdom
Always comes with grey hair.

NURSE

I am forbearing a bit and they wound me
With this stinging speech.
Do you intend to insult me endlessly?

CHARITE

I respect your old age
But Cadmus and the princess
Are coming to these parts.
Let's not disturb their goodbyes.

(Exit Charite and Nurse in one direction. Enter Cadmus and Hermione from another.)

CADMUS

Beautiful Hermione, I'm going to part;

I am going to execute what Love directs me to do.
Despite the peril which awaits me,
I intend to deliver you or destroy myself.
I see you, at last, I am telling you that I love you.
It's enough so as to die satisfied.

HERMIONE

Ah! Cadmus, why do you love me?
Why do you want to seek a very certain death?
Eh! What can human valor
Do against the God Mars in wrath?
See into what perils your love drags us!
I ought to prefer your hate.
Ah! Cadmus, why do you love me?

CADMUS

You love me; it suffices; don't be pained any further.
My destiny, whatever it may be, can only be sweet.

HERMIONE

Let's live to love each other, and stop pursuing
The funereal plan you have formed.
It ought to be really sweet to live
When one loves and one is loved.

CADMUS

I see you enslaved under an unjust law.
Is it loving you to suffer it?

When what one loves is exposed to perish,
The most frightful death is to be envied.

HERMIONE

But you cannot think there's going to be life?
For my life mustn't you be without terror?
I will live under unjust sway
To which my cruel destiny delivers me,
But if you perish for me
I cannot survive you.

CADMUS

I need succor; do you want to overwhelm me?
Ah, princess, is it time to make me tremble?

HERMIONE

Be sensitive to my alarms.

CADMUS

I feel your sorrows only too much.

HERMIONE

Will you leave despite my crying?

CADMUS

It's necessary to dry up the source of your tears.

HERMIONE

What! You are going to leave me?

CADMUS

I am going to help you.

HERMIONE

Ah! You are going to perish!
You are seeking out a horrible death.
My heart tells me too well that you will lose the day.

CADMUS

The love I have for you believes nothing's impossible.
As I leave, it flatters me with a happy return.

CADMUS AND HERMIONE

Believe in my love.

HERMIONE

You are not listening to my tenderness!
Nothing can restrain you!

CADMUS

Time presses.

TOGETHER

In the name of the most beautiful fetters love has made,
Live, if you love me.

CADMUS

Let's hope.

HERMIONE

All causes me despair.
How I wish myself ill for
Having known too well how to please you!

TOGETHER

How a tender love costs sorrows!

HERMIONE

You are fleeing?

CADMUS

Have to.

HERMIONE

Stay.

CADMUS

I cannot.
The more I delay, the more I weaken;
I must tear myself from this place.

HERMIONE

Ah, Cadmus!

CADMUS

Hermione!

TOGETHER

Goodbye!

(Cadmus leaves.)

HERMIONE

(alone) Love, see what ill you make for us,
Where are the blessings you promised?
Didn't you pity our pains?
Your most inhumane rigors,
Will they always be for the most tender hearts?
Cruel love, for whom are you reserving your sweetness?

LOVE

(on a cloud) Calm your discontent, dissipate your fears;
Love is coming to dry your tears.
He doesn't abandon those who follow his laws;
Remember that for me all is possible.
Thus nothing remains insensitive to my approach.
Thus, to divert it, everything vivifies at my voice's call.

(The statues animated by Love jump from their pedestals to dance. Love descends and comes to sing in the midst of the animated statues.)

LOVE

Stop complaining
Of suffering from loving.
Lovers, you mustn't fear anything.
If you are suffering, your reward is charming.
After inhuman rigors
You love without pains;
You laugh at the jealous.
A blessing full of charms
Which costs tears
Becomes more sweet.
All must render homage
To the amorous empire.
Sooner or later you have to get involved.
Without loving anything, you cannot be happy.
After inhuman rigors, etc.

(Love resumes his place on the cloud which bears him, the statues return to their pedestals, while ten little golden cherubs holding baskets full of flowers are in their turn animated by Love and come at his direction to cast their flowers as they fly around Hermione.)

LOVE

Loves, come sow a thousand flowers under her feet.

HERMIONE

Leave me my sorrow, I find attractions
In the horror of an intense peril.
Is this the help that they must offer me?
Perhaps the one I love
Is already near perishing.

LOVE

(flying in the midst of ten cherubs)

I am going to aid him.

CURTAIN

ACT III

FIRST TYRIAN PRINCE

You are really turning your glance away?

SECOND TYRIAN PRINCE

Are you afraid of the dragon of Mars?

ARBAS

Precaution is necessary.
It's wise to foresee an irritating accident.
One mustn't march here with temerity.

FIRST PRINCE

It's very proper to be prudent.

ARBAS

I am bold when need be.
If anyone doubts it, he'll able to learn.

SECOND PRINCE

Who would want to attack you?

FIRST PRINCE

One would take you valiant on your word,
But the color of your face
Responds ill to your valor.

ARBAS

Is it by color
That one ought to judge courage!

SECOND PRINCE

How disturbed your nerves appear!
You're trembling.

ARBAS

That's the way it seems to you.
Each believes whatever resembles himself,
Perhaps it's you who are trembling.
May funereal love be cursed
Which brings us so much suffering on this unlucky
   day!
It's a relief to curse
And it's hard to know how to curse love too much.

THE TWO PRINCES TOGETHER

Let's beware of ever having wanted
To be amorous.
Of all the ills of life,
Love is the most dangerous.

FIRST PRINCE

Cadmus is going to try to render Mars propitious.
It's here that he intends to offer a sacrifice.

SECOND PRINCE

For different duties we must separate.

THE PRINCES

(together) Let's go prepare everything.

(The Princes leave.)

ARBAS

Let's acquit ourselves of the duties Cadmus assigned us.
What an uproar! No, it's nothing; courage friends, courage.
What trouble to give courage while trembling.
It's not my fault if I am not valiant.
I try at least to appear so.
I am not the only one who prides himself on being so,

And who only seems to be.
We must fetch some water for the ceremony.
Advance, I am with you. What a furious dragon!

THE TWO AFRICANS

O god! O god!

(As the two Africans go to fetch water, the dragon hurls himself on them and drags them away.)

ARBAS

Ah! My life is done for!
Isn't there a tree or a rock
Which is open for me to hide in?

CADMUS

(entering) Where are you going?

ARBAS

The dragon.

CADMUS

Well?

ARBAS

Ah! My dear master

CADMUS

Speak up.

ARBAS

The dragon.

CADMUS

Whereabouts do you see him appear?
I'm looking everywhere and I don't see him.

ARBAS

What! The dragon's fleeing us?
Why, are you looking carefully?

CADMUS

Where are your companions?
What is keeping you so silent?
You appear speechless with terror.

ARBAS

Lord, you judge wrongly of me.
If I am speechless, it's only with rage.
Alas! My poor companions.
The dragon made a snack of them.

CADMUS

Let's go, I must avenge them.

ARBAS

Why in such a hurry for the dragon to eat you?
Let it hide. Ah! There it comes!
Help! Help! I am dead, I am dead!
O heaven, where will be my asylum?
Terror renders me motionless;
I don't know how to take another step.
Ah! Let's hide, don't breath.

(Arbas hides and Cadmus battles against the dragon.)

CADMUS

(after having killed the dragon) I can no longer put off
Addressing the God Mars to calm his rage.
If I can soften him, nothing can disturb me.
My men are scattered; they must be reassembled.

(Exit Cadmus.)

ARBAS

(leaving the spot where he was hiding)
The dragon, satiated with blood and carnage,
Has at last retired to some savage cave.
Everything is calm around here and I no longer hear
    anything.

I feel my courage coming back
And believe I can safely flee.
Let's go recount everywhere the death of my master.
Ah, how I pity his funereal fate!
Let's go; but what am I seeing appear?
The dragon stretched out! Isn't he dead?
No, I see him pierced, his blood is flowing; ah, the traitor!
I cannot control my wrath against him.
And I want to give him at least the last blows.

(Arbas takes his sword in his hand and goes to pierce the dragon which again makes a movement that forces Arbas to beat a retreat.)

FIRST PRINCE

(entering) What! Sword in hand!
What must he be attempting?

SECOND PRINCE

With what peril are you threatened?

THE TWO PRINCES

(together) We will take care to protect you.

ARBAS

You are coming a bit late; the peril has passed.

THE TWO PRINCES

What do we see? Who would have believed it!
What? The dragon is beaten?

ARBAS

We are bringing back the victory without you.

FIRST PRINCE

Did you follow Cadmus?

SECOND PRINCE

Did you share in his glory?

ARBAS

Eh! We weren't far off when he was battling.

THE TWO PRINCES

Tell us about this battle.

ARBAS

I am so out of breath from it
That as yet, I can hardly express myself except with
 pain.
It's good to dry this embloodied sword
For fear it will be spoiled.

THE TWO PRINCES

Ah! What shame for us to miss the opportunity
To display our courage.

ARBAS

All these pains and regrets
Are over duties which do not cost anything;
When one no longer sees anything to do,
It's necessary to brave the breeze a bit.

FIRST PRINCE

Watch out for yourself a bit;
Cadmus will do us justice.
But he's coming; let's fall in to see the sacrifice.

(Cadmus enters with the High Priest, two singing priests, a Drummer, six dancing priests. Two priests bear a great trophy which covers the High Priest as he moves center stage.)

HIGH PRIEST

Mars! Oh, you who can,
When you choose, unchain
The furies of war;
O Mars! Receive our prayers.

CHORUS OF PRIESTS

O Mars! Receive our prayers.

THE HIGH PRIEST

Your funereal wrath is not less dangerous
Than the fatal outburst of thunder.
O Mars! Receive our prayers

CHORUS OF PRIESTS

O Mars! Receive our prayers.

THE HIGH PRIEST

Bloody battles are your sports.
When it pleases you, you know how to fill the whole earth
With frightful ravages.
O Mars! Receive our prayers.

CHORUS

O Mars! Receive our prayers.

(The singing priests remain prostrated, and the dancing priests make yet another entrance to the sound of drums and the clash of arms; after which the singing priests rise and sing.)

HIGH PRIEST

Formidable Mars!
Indomitable Mars!
O Mars! O Mars! O Mars!

CHORUS

Formidable Mars!
Indomitable Mars!
O Mars! O Mars! O Mars!

HIGH PRIEST

O pitiless Mars,
Is your implacable hate
Revocable?
Must it overwhelm
An unshakable soul
In the midst of dangers?

CHORUS

O Mars! O Mars! O Mars!
Formidable Mars!
Indomitable Mars!
O Mars! O Mars! O Mars!

HIGH PRIEST

Let the tumult of alarms,
Let the uproar, let the clash,

Let the tumult of arms,
Resound everywhere.

CHORUS

O Mars! O Mars! O Mars!
Formidable Mars!
Indomitable Mars!
O Mars! O Mars! O Mars!

HIGH PRIEST

Let them bring the victim forward.
Let it calm the wrath which animates you
And draw on us only your softest glances!

CHORUS

O Mars! O Mars! O Mars!
Formidable Mars!
Indomitable Mars!
O Mars! O Mars! O Mars!

(Mars appears in his chariot and interrupts the sacrifice.)

MARS

It's vain to hope
That useless prayers will appease my wrath.
I am not revoking my laws.
If Cadmus wants to satisfy me,

Let him manage, if he can, to deserve my choice.
A vain respect cannot please me.
One doesn't satisfy Mars except through great exploits.
You that hell nourishes,
Come, cruel furies,
Come, break the altar into a hundred scattered pieces.

CHORUS

O Mars! O Mars! O Mars!

(Four furies descend and demolish the altar, then fly off each holding an ember of the sacrifice in hand. The chariot of Mars turns at the same time and carries him to the back of the stage where he is lost from view, and all the priests and assistants withdraw, shouting, "O Mars!")

CURTAIN

ACT IV

The stage represents the field of Mars.

CADMUS

Here's the field of Mars;
Here, without delay
I must finish my attempt.
I have the teeth of the dragon, I am going to sow them.

ARBAS

These are enemies you will see take form,
So many armed soldiers are going to be born,
That at first you will be overwhelmed by their blows.
And perhaps you aren't thinking
That you have only me here alone with you.

CADMUS

I don't wish to expose anyone
To the peril to which I am abandoning myself.
I must fight alone, and retain only you.
You know my love, I am sure of your faith;

I really want you to be the last to leave me.

ARBAS

Lord, you honor me more than I deserve.

CADMUS

If I am making only a vain effort,
Accomplish what I direct you.
As soon as you know of my death,
Hasten to see Hermione;
Go, bring her my last prayers.
Let her live, it suffices to pity an unfortunate.
Let her take care to keep the faithful memory
Of a flame so beautiful.
It's the unique reward that I desire
For what I shall have done for her.
I don't intend to detain you any longer.
Leave me.

ARBAS

Must I leave you?

CADMUS

I insist on it; obey.

ARBAS

Ah! What violence,

Lord, you exact from my obedience!

(Arbas leaves.)

LOVE

(appearing on a brilliant cloud)

Cadmus, receive the gift that I am coming to bring to you.
It's the work of God who forges thunder.
Don't fail to throw it
In the middle of soldiers borne from the Earth.
Today you must reveal
What a great heart seconded by Love can do.
Complete the plan in which my ardor binds you.

CADMUS

I am going to obey you without further delay.

LOVE AND CADMUS

You must reveal today
What a great heart seconded by Love can do.

(Love flies off, and Cadmus sows the teeth of the dragon from which the earth produces armed soldiers, and which prepare right away to turn their weapons on Cadmus; but he throws into their midst like a grenade, what Love brought him, which breaks into several splinters and which inspires the combatants with a furor to fight each other and to strangle themselves. Eight armed soldiers born of the earth battle. The last five who remain alive come to bring their arms to the feet of Cadmus.)

ECHION

(fighting) Let's stop a funereal distraction.
Why are we immolating ourselves as we are born here-
  abouts?
Let's reserve the blood that remains to us
To serve a hero favored by the gods.

CADMUS

Go, let each of you in these walls rush
To render homage to the princess,
Who must here give you absolute orders.
Your first respects are owed to her.
I will follow you closely; it's my strongest wish.

(The combatants obey Cadmus who remains to reassemble the Tyrians.)

CADMUS

Let's find our Tyrians; they are trembling for my life.
Let's go reassure them; let's look every where.

GIANT

(entering) No, it's not enough to have satisfied Mars;

You see an enemy you must also fight;
Instead of triumphing, resume the battle.

CADMUS

Let's battle.

GIANT

I pity the peril you are running.
It's shameful for me to conquer with so much advantage.
Go flee, and give up to me the object of our loves.
You no longer have gods who are protecting your life.

CADMUS

The gods have given me courage
And that's aid enough.

GIANT

We'll see if there's nothing that astonishes you.
Let them come to me, let them surround him,
Let him be pierced on all sides.

PALLAS

(seated on a flying owl)

Cadmus, shut your eyes, perfidious ones, stop!

(Pallas discovers her shield and presents it to the eyes of the four giants, who remain motionless, and in a moment become four statues.)

PALLAS

See, Cadmus, see that death
Has punished their injustice.

CADMUS

What do I see? The armed giants
Are no longer living bodies!

PALLAS

I promised you my assistance
I am going to prepare a superb palace for you.
I wish to join to the sweetness of a marriage full of allures
Dazzle and magnificence.
In peace, experience a glorious fate.
Go, don't listen to anything but the love that animates you.
Hermione is coming here.

CADMUS

How must I express my thanks?

PALLAS

(flying off) To protect the virtue of a magnanimous prince
Is the sweetest function of the gods.

(Pallas leaves. Hermione enters.)

CADMUS

My princess!

HERMIONE

Cadmus!

CADMUS

What joy!

HERMIONE

What glory!

CADMUS

At last I see you free!

HERMIONE

I see you again victor!

CADMUS

What a favorable victory!

HERMIONE

How much it cost my heart.

CADMUS

It's a charming privilege
To be able to save from cruel slavery
The beauty by whom one is charmed!

HERMIONE

What a fate worthy of envy
To be able to owe the happiness of her life
To the hand of a beloved conqueror.

CADMUS AND HERMIONE

After inhuman rigors
Heaven favors our prayers.
Ah! How sweet is the memory
Of pains, once one is happy!

(A cloud rises from the ground and envelops Hermione.)

JUNO

(on a peacock) You see the effect of my wrath;

You must again battle Juno and her power.
The care my unfaithful spouse takes for you
Attracts on your passion the outburst of my vengeance.
Raise Hermione on your ark before his eyes.
Execute instantly what Juno orders you.

HERMIONE

(atop a rainbow) O heaven!

ALL TOGETHER

O heaven! O Heaven! Hermione! Hermione!

CURTAIN

ACT V

The scene represents the palace that Pallas had prepared for the wedding of Cadmus and Hermione.

CADMUS

(alone) Alas, beautiful Hermione!
Can I be happy without you?
What's the use of this pomp
They're preparing for me in this palace?
All hope is lost for us.
The happiness of a love so rare and faithful
Even amongst the gods excited jealousy.
Alas, beautiful Hermione!
Can I be happy without you?
We were flattered that our barbarous fate
Had exhausted its wrath.
What harshness, when they separate
Two hearts so close to being joined in such sweet fetters!
Alas, beautiful Hermione!
Can I be happy without you?

PALLAS

(on her cloud) Your prayers are going to be satisfied;
Jupiter and Juno have ended their quarrel.
Love himself made peace between them.
Your Hermione is finally coming down to this palace.
The gods are coming with her.
Heaven intends that this day be celebrated forever.

(The heavens open and all the gods appear, coming forward to accompany Hermione, who descends on a throne at the side of Hymen who gives his place to Cadmus and puts himself amidst the two spouses. Troupes of divinities, as many in heaven as on earth. The followers of Cadmus and Hermione come to take part in the rejoicing of the gods, and Jupiter begins to invite the heavens and earth to contribute to the happiness of these two lovers.)

JUPITER

Whoever follows the laws of the master of thunder,
Let heaven and earth
Agree to fulfill their vows.
After so harsh a fate,
After so many cruel pains,
Faithful lovers
Live happily.

ALL THE CHORUS

(answering)

After so harsh a fate,
After so many cruel pains,
Faithful lovers
Live happily.

HYMEN [MARRIAGE]

Hymen wants to offer you his most beautiful fetters.

JUNO

Juno wants to form the bonds.

CHORUS

Faithful lovers
Live happily.

VENUS

Venus will give you eternal delights.

MARS

I will divert fatal quarrels and dangerous enemies from you.

CHORUS

Faithful lovers
Live happily.

PALLAS

Expect from Pallas a thousand new favors.

LOVE

Love will forever conserve such fine passions.

CHORUSES

After so harsh a fate,
After so many cruel pains,
Faithful lovers
Live happily.

JUPITER

Here, Hymen, take care here of dances and sports.

CHORUSES

Faithful lovers
Live happily.

HYMEN

Come, god of feasts, pleasant games, come,

Heap your delights on these lucky spouses
While all heaven prepares
The gifts that it destined for them.
Earth must mix in it its rarest possessions.
Come, god of feasts; pleasant games, come,
Heap your delights on these lucky spouses.

(Comus dances alone. Four followers of Comus. Four hamadryads emerge from the earth with baskets full of fruits. Comus begins to dance alone.)

ARBAS AND NURSE

Shall we remain in silence,
When they're dancing, when they're singing?
Sorrow has had its time,
Heaven has forever driven it off,
Pleasures have taken its place.
When two hearts are constant
Sooner or later they'll be satisfied.
How sweet it is, to sigh
After emerging from a long martyrdom!
Sorrow has had its time,
Heaven has forever driven it off.
Pleasures have taken its place.
When two hearts are constant
Sooner or later they'll be satisfied.

(Cherub-cupids make gifts from the gods descend from heaven, under a sort of little pavilion attached to elegant chains. The hamadryads and the followers of

Comus bring them to the spouses and form a dance in which Charite mixes a song.)

CHARITE

Lovers, love your fetters,
Your cares and your sighs;
Love measures your pleasures
By your pains.
He causes alarms,
He dearly sells his charms,
But for such a great blessing
All your ills are nothing.
Without a pleasant passion
Life has no attractions.
Who can touch a soul
Untouched by love?
He causes alarms,
He dearly sells his charms,
Bur for such a great blessing
All your ills are nothing.

(All the gods of heaven and earth resume singing. The hamadryads and the followers of Comus continue to dance, and the mixture of singing and dancing forms a general rejoicing which ends the feast of the marriage of Cadmus and Hermione.)

ALL THE CHORUSES

After so harsh a fate,

After so many cruel pains,
Faithful lovers
Live happily.

CURTAIN

PERSEUS
A PLAY IN FIVE ACTS

For Horvalis

CAST OF CHARACTERS

Phronine, follower of Virtue

Megathynie, another follower of virtue

Troupe of Male followers of Virtue

Troupe of Female followers of Virtue

Innocence

The Pleasure of Innocence

Fortune

Magnificence

Abundance

Troupe of Male followers of Fortune

Troupe of Female followers of Fortune

PERSEUS, son of Jupiter and Diana, lover of Andromeda.

CEPHEUS, King of Ethipia.

CASSIOPIA, Queen and spouse of Cepheus

MEROPE, sister of Cassiopia

ANDROMEDA, only daughter of Cepheus and Cassiopia.

PHINEAS, brother of Cepheus to whom Andromeda was promised.

TROUPE of followers of Cepheus

TROUPE of followers of Cassiopia

TROUPE of ETHIOPIAN Men and Women

Quadrille of Four young men chosen to battle over the prizes of Juno's games.

QUADRILLE of Four young girls chosen for the same games.

AMPHIMEDON

CORETE

PROTENOR

MERCURY

TROUPE OF CYCLOPSES

TROUPE of NYMPHS in the suite of PALLAS

MEDUSA. A Gorgon

EURYALE, A Gorgon

STENONE, a Gorgon

TROUPE of Monsters formed from Medusa's blood.

IDAS, one of the courtiers of Cepheus

TROUE of SAILORS

TROUPE of Female SAILORS

HIGH PRIEST of the God Hymen

The Suite of the Grand Priest

TROUPE of Courtiers of CEPHEUS

TROUPE of COMBATANTS on the side of PHINEAS

TROUPE of COMBATANTS on the side of CEPHEUS and PERSEUS

VENUS

CUPID

TROUPE of CUPIDS

HYMEN

THE GRACES

THE SPORTS

PROLOGUE

A thicket.

PHRONINE

Virtue intends to choose this place for her retreat.
It's a lucky region. Everything here pleases my eyes.

MEGATHYME

Virtue causes secret felicity to be found
In the saddest spots.

PHRONINE

Without Virtue, without her help
You don't have anything real
She's always lovable
She must always be loved.

MEGATHYNE

She perpetuates the memory
Of a hero who follows her.
The glory to which Virtue leads

Is perfect glory.

PHRONINE and MEGATHYNE

Let's follow on her heels everywhere
One cannot know her
Without loving her attractions
There can be no happiness
Where Virtue is absent

(Virtue comes forward in the midst of a troupe of servants of both sexes. Innocence and Innocent Pleasures accompany Virtue.)

PHRONINE, MEGATHYNE, and CHORUS

O charming Virtue
Your empire is sweet
With you all are satisfied
One is not happy without you
Your empire is sweet.

VIRTUE

Don't abuse yourself to such a degree by a vain hope
They cost a thousand efforts, they make thousands
    jealous.
Fickle Fortune to injure me is constant
When he follows my steps people are exposed to his
    blows.
You find in his fatal wrath,

A hydra always reborn.

MEGATHYNE

With you, nothing is shocking.

PHRONINE

One is not happy without you.

MEGATHYNE, PHRONINE and THE CHORUS

O charming Virtue, etc.

VIRTUE

Let's flee from the embarrassing ceremonies of grandeur
A retreat has blessings whose gentleness enchants
And that are reserved for us.
Let's enjoy the happiness of an innocent life
That's the greatest blessing of all.

MEGATHYNE, PHRONINE, and The CHORUS

O charming Virtue, etc.

(Innocence, the Innocent Pleasures and all of Virtue's suite express their joy by dancing and singing.)

PHRONINE and MEGATHYNE

Brilliant grandeur
Which causes such commotion
Has nothing that tempts us
Repose flees it.
Unlucky ones who follow her
Flighty Fortune
Leave us in peace!
You never give
Anything except a pompous slavery
All your wealth, has only false attractions.
We restrict our desires.
Our fate is tranquil
It's a blessing which ought to make us happy.
Virtue crowns
Her constant lovers
Their prayers will be satisfied.
Fickle Fortune, etc.

(The rustic site that virtue has chosen for a retreat is suddenly embellished with magnificent ornamentation. From the earth emerges a square of flowers, two rows of golden statues with golden cradles and gushing fountains.)

VIRTUE

Who's causing us to see so much magnificence here?
It's Fortune who's coming forward.

(The dazzling commotion of a large number of instruments is heard. Fortune approaches. Abundance and Magnificence accompany him, with a richly bedecked following.)

VIRTUE

Do you seek me when I flee you?
Fortune, I know too well that you vex me.
No, it's not an effort you ordinarily make
To embellish the places where I am.

FORTUNE

Let's efface the past's unfortunate memory.
I've always battled against your vanity.
An august hero orders that Fortune
Be at peace with Virtue.

VIRTUE

Ah! I recognize him with no difficulty.
He's the hero who calmed the universe.

FORTUNE

He alone could vanquish my hate of you.
He reveres you and I serve him.
I love him faithfully, I who am so fickle.
I rush everywhere, ardently following his desires.
You always seem so strict.
Yet you are still his most cherished love.

VIRTUE

My most brilliant gifts are less than yours.
You find so many hearts who adore only you.
You enchant almost all of theirs.

FORTUNE

You reign over a heart which, by itself, is worth more than all others.
Ah, if he'd wanted to follow me, he could have surmounted all.
All would tremble, all would yield to the passion that enthuses him.
It's you, extremely magnificent Virtue,
It's you who stopped him.

VIRTUE

His great heart revealed itself better.
It has a genuine effect over him.
He intends to make the world happy
He prefers to become the master of joy
The glory of showing that he deserves to be.

VIRTUE and FORTUNE

Let's fight endlessly to see who better serves
This glorious hero.

VIRTUE, FORTUNE and CHORUS

The Gods gave him simply for the happiness of the world.
May his works be great! May his destiny be fine!
In a profound peace
He finds a fertile Spring
Of new triumphs.
The Gods gave him simply for the happiness of the world.

VIRTUE

Even in these sports everything speaks to him of us.
The Gods who are contemplating their most perfect work
In former times by tracing the image of Perseus
I shall see to it that Apollo revives him today.

VIRTUE and FORTUNE

A thousand new concerts ought to be heard
All promise a favorable fate to merit.
What blessings must not attend
Our happy agreement.

(The followers of Virtue and the Followers of Fortune join together, and express their joy in their dances and their songs.)

THE FOLLOWERS OF VIRTUE AND FORTUNE

What a lucky day for us!
Everything's going the way we wish
What a lucky day for us!
How sweet is our fate.
Virtue sees all of her followers in peace.
Fortune, for them, withholds his fatal wrath.
What a lucky day for us.
All our life will be happy, taste, taste life.
Nothing disturbs our plans, Heaven fulfills our wishes.
What a lucky day for us, etc.

VIRTUE, FORTUNE and THE CHORUS

Happy intelligence
Gentle, charming peace
Fulfill our hopes.
Gentle, charming peace.
Would you could last forever.

CURTAIN

ACT I

A magnificently decorated public square prepared to celebrate games in honor of Juno.

CEPHEUS

My only fear is that Juno may refuse
To appease her hate against us.
I fear that frightful Medusa, despite our prayers,
May return to serve her funeral wrath.
In vain is Ethiopia submissive to my sway
What hope am I allowed,
If heaven is always armed against us?
Against this frightful monster my nation is defenseless
Whoever sees her is suddenly transformed into a rock.
And if Juno doesn't stop her vengeance that your pride offended
I will soon be the king of a lifeless nation.

CASSIOPIA

Lucky spouse, lucky mother
Very vain of a glorious fate

I've been unable to prevent myself from exciting the wrath
Of the spouse of the God of Earth and Heaven.
I compared my glory to her immortal glory.
The Goddess is punishing my criminal pride.
But I hope to appease her strict wrath.
I'm opening these celebratory games
That have been prepared hereabouts in Juno's honor.
My pride offended this divinity.
My respect must repair
My vanity's crime.

CEPHEUS

I'm going with Perseus to implore the help
Of the God from whom he derives his birth.
He's the son of the greatest of the Gods.
Appease the fatal wrath of Juno
That there should be hereabouts
An odious object.
Like a son of her rival.

CASSIOPIA

By a cruel punishment
The Gods have made us see their hate.
Easily irritated
They are appeased with difficulty.

CEPHEUS

The Gods punish pride!
It's not grandeur that irritates heaven.
It abases when it chooses, and reduces to powder.
But a prompt repentance
Can stop the lightning
Quite ready to strike,

MEROPE

Would we could disarm Heaven that threatens us.

CEPHEUS, CASSIOPIA, and MEROPE
O Gods! Who punish audacity!
Gods! formidable enemies!
We ask mercy of you!
Pardon submissive hearts.

(Exit Cepheus)

CASSIOPIA

Phineas is destined to marry my daughter
You know my plans for you,
My sister, by your marriage it would have been nice for me
To join Perseus to my family.
But I wish it in vain. Love won't consent to it.
In the eyes of this hero, my daughter has great attractions.

MEROPE

The son of Jupiter adores her.
Do you imagine that I am yet
To notice it?
I take too much interest in it not to know it.
I was enjoying a happy peace
Before this hero appeared in this court.
By a deceitful hope
I almost delivered myself to the power of love.

CASSIOPIA

Indeed hide the weakness in which your heart is taken

MEROPE

Even today, my conqueror
Is still unaware of the funereal slavery of my heart.
I would die of shame and rage
If the ingrate were to know the love I have for him.

CASSIOPIA

With shame and rage
Your heart is torn apart.
You lose hope of pleasing.
Can one be so soon defeated
By a despairing passion?
Call on scorn, let your passion give way.
Emerge with its help from so fatal a torture.

MEROPE

Sad help! A remedy
More cruel than the illness.

CASSIOPIA

To supervise the games I must leave.
Your sorrow is irritated by my advice.

CASSIOPIA and MEROPE

Time alone can cure
The ills that passion makes you suffer.

(Cassiopia leaves)

MEROPE

Ah, I will guard my heart carefully
If I can get it back.
Come, just scorn, come, it's a long wait.
Break these harsh chains;
Hasten to give me back
The gentle charm of my just repose.
Ah! I will guard my heart
If I can get it back.
Alas, my heart sighs, and that sigh is very tender.
Go! Despite my scorn recall my languishing;
Love is still my conqueror
And in vain I want to protect myself against it.
Ah! I engaged my heart too deeply,

I can no longer get it back.
Andromeda's coming to see the games.
Phineas is coming forward with her.
The hope for their marriage still flatters my prayers.
And that's my last hope.

ANDROMEDA and PHINEAS

(entering.)

Trust me, trust me.

ANDROMEDA

Stop being afraid.

PHINEAS

Stop feigning.

ANDROMEDA

I want to love you; I must.

PHINEAS

You don't love me, I can see it.

ANDROMEDA

Stop worrying.

PHINEAS

Stop pretending.

ANDROMEDA and PHINEAS

Trust me, trust me.

MEROPE

You are both so lovable
And the two of you both love each other.
What differences are capable
Of breaking such bonds?
What wouldn't wretched lovers endure
If passion has ills for happy lovers?

ANDROMEDA

For no reason his chagrin explodes.

PHINEAS

Shall I lose my sweetest hope without chagrin?
Condemn an ingrate.

ANDROMEDA

Condemn a jealous lover.

PHINEAS

Perseus pleases her and with vain excuses
She intends to blind my outraged love.
She loved me. No, I'm abusing myself.
No, since she changed so soon?
Her heart's never been really engaged to mine.

ANDROMEDA

Duty gives you a just empire over my heart.
You ought not to fear a fatal change.
A lover, assured of the happiness he desires,
Can he be jealous of a wretched rival?

PHINEAS

No, I cannot suffer him to share a chain
Whose weight appears so charming to me.
If you were to overwhelm him with the cruelest torture,
I would be jealous of his pain.
But I don't see dazzling scorn.
If he's so wretched, his constancy astonishes me.
Love that hope abandons
Is less calm and less constant.

ANDROMEDA

What pleasure can you take in troubling yourself?
And by what can your love be alarmed?

I flee your rival with extreme care.
Is one accustomed
To flee what one loves?

PHINEAS

You pursue glory and duty with regret.
By fleeing a lover more agreeable to your eyes.
You found him formidable
Since you are afraid to see him.

ANDROMEDA

Everything frights you, everything irritates you.
You are teaching me to fear a glorious hero.
I don't see his merit.
Do you want your importunate suspicion to open my eyes?

PHINEAS

Ah, if you flatter him with the slightest hope
The God that you believe to be the author of his birth
Ought to make his wrath blaze forth,
If he doesn't want to know my jealous distraction.

ANDROMEDA

Just heaven!

PHINEAS

You are trembling! Perseus pleases you.
If his peril can make you tremble.

ANDROMEDA

Heaven is only too much enraged
And you are braving a God who can crush you.
It's for you I must tremble.

PHINEAS

Don't resort to trickery.

ANDROMEDA

Don't do me an injustice.
I want to love you; I must.

PHINEAS

You don't love me, I see it.

ANDROMEDA

Stop worrying.

PHINEAS

Stop pretending.

ANDROMEDA and PHINEAS

Trust me, trust me.

MEROPE

He's as much afraid as he is in love.
Ah, how many alarms love causes
Ah, how much attraction love would have
If it never troubled lovers.

MEROPE, ANDROMEDA, PHINEAS

With the sweetness of her charms!
Ah, how much attraction love would have
If one always could love in peace.

ANDROMEDA

My duty is for you; my duty can suffice
To give you tranquil hope.

PHINEAS

Are you going to talk of duty forever?
Does love have nothing to say to me?

ANDROMEDA

The games are going to begin.
Let's place ourselves where we can see them.

(Cassiopia returns with a troupe of servants who bring prizes. Quadrilles of young people chosen for the games, a Chorus of spectators.)

CASSIOPIA

O Juno, powerful Goddess
That one cannot revere enough!
In your name I assemble these engaging youths
Let the sleeping torch of marriage soon light.
Each is going to demonstrate his skill
To contest for the prizes I have had prepared.
Don't keep an implacable hate for us.
If pride renders me guilty.
I've recognized my crime and wish to repair it.
See with a favorable glance
The games we are going to celebrate in your honor.

CHORUS

Let your wrath calm,
O Juno, fulfill our prayers
If we succeed in pleasing you
Let us be happy.

(They begin the games contesting for the dancing prize)

AMPHIMEDON

Flee! Your prayers are vain and Juno rejects them.

Of new misfortunes, in converted rocks,
We are only too well forewarned!
That Medusa's going to be seen.

CORITES

Medusa's returning to these parts!

PROTEUS

Let's beware of seeing her; death is in her eyes.

ALL

(fleeing) Let's flee this terrible monster
Let's escape if possible.
Let's escape; let's hasten our steps.
Let's flee a horrid death.

CURTAIN

ACT II

The gardens of the palace of Cepheus.

CASSIOPIA

Must all heaven interest itself against us?
Gods, can I ever hope to soften you?

PHINEAS

I've led the prisoners here.

MEROPE

Perseus has brought the King into the palace.

PHINEAS

Medusa's withdrawing; she's leaving us in peace.

CASSIOPIA

She can return, she can surprise us.
Juno is stubborn about avenging herself
Against her, none of the Gods can help us.

My only hope is to entice
Jupiter to protect us.

PHINEAS

I hear you. I know what your hope is.
Perseus has vainly boasted of his divine birth.
After your promise, after the King's choice
Andromeda must be mine.

CASSIOPIA

Heaven's punishing my crime; it is inexorable.
I need help in my mortal terror.

PHINEAS

Ah, if heaven is fair
Will you be found less culpable
If you break your faith with me?

MEROPE

He is loved by the one he loves.
You've approved his prayers
Will you break the bonds
That you yourself have forged?
How terrifying is despair.
For an extreme passion
He flatters himself on being happy!

PHINEAS and MEROPE

Will you break the bonds
That you yourself have forged?

(Cepheus enters with his suite.)

PHINEAS

Lord, you've destined me
To the fortunate marriage
With lovable Andromeda.
They want me to give way to the passion of Perseus.
Would you take from me a blessing you've given me?

CEPHEUS

To the Son of Jupiter one can give way without shame.

PHINEAS

And you believe the fairy-tale he tells you?
Do you imagine that a sovereign God
Who presides over the universe
Allows himself through passion to change into liquid gold
To secretly enter a bronze tower?
For this imaginary prodigy
Perseus is revered by vulgar credulity.
He calls himself the Son of God whose sway heaven obeys.
But I don't pretend to believe that on his oath.

CEPHEUS

Your incredulity shall have no further excuse,
My brother
his valor is going to open your eyes.
Recognize the son of the most powerful of gods.
He is offering to cut off the head of Medusa.

MEROPE, CASSIOPIA and PHINEAS

The head of Medusa! Oh, heavens!

CEPHEUS

My daughter is the reward he demands.

CASSIOPIA and CEPHEUS

What price can be too great to pay this glorious effort?

PHINEAS

Success is not certain; permit me to await it.
Allow my passion to protect itself from
Abandoning so precious a blessing.
Perseus is not yet victorious.

(Phineas leaves)

CEPHEUS

Hope ought to be reborn in our hearts

Gods, let Juno engage to serve her wrath.
Irritated Gods, be appeased!
Heaven's vengeance has known only too well how to appear.
The Son of Jupiter is going to fight for us.
O Heaven, favor the son of your master.

(The three repeat the last two verses, then Cepheus and Cassiopia leave.)

MEROPE

Ah, he's going to perish! Must I tremble for him? Why?
Why have I taken so much fright for the lover of Andromeda?
Must my scorn be forgotten?
What interest do I have in his life?
He will live for another; he's lost to me.
Yet when I think of his extreme peril
When I see him seek a horrible death
Without thinking that he doesn't love me
I merely feel that I love him.

(Enter Andromeda)

ANDROMEDA

Unfortunates, that a frightful monster
Has changed to rocks with its terrible glance,
You no longer feel your harsh fate,
And your hardened hearts are forever at peace.

Alas, feeling hearts
Are a thousand times more unfortunate.

MEROPE

(aside) Andromeda seems speechless.
She's come to dream in these parts.
Ah, I recognize in her eyes
The same concern that is agitating me.

ANDROMEDA

He just loves me too much, and everything solicits me
To love him in my turn.
He received life from the great gods.
Passion hurls him into our mortal perils.
How to hold out against so much merit
And against so much love?

MEROPE

(to Andromeda) Ah! You love Perseus! He causes you
    alarms.
Don't disavow your tears over him.
Your tender feelings are very plain.
You love him.

ANDROMEDA

You love him.
Hope of marriage has charmed your soul.
And I know the plans you had erected;

I see that scorn doesn't extinguish your flame.
Perseus is ruining himself, and you are alarmed.
You love him.

ANDROMEDA and MEROPE

Ah, how a tender heart is to be pitied;
To be reduced to feigning.
What torment does it not suffer?
A wretched love that it cannot extinguish
And who dares reveal it?
Ah, how a tender heart is to be pitied;
To be reduced to feigning.

MEROPE

It's true; scorn vainly wants to inspire me.
I feel pity disarming my rage.
Perseus is an ingrate who cannot love me.
He doesn't allow himself to please me. Alas, he loves
    you, too much.
How could you help but love him?

ANDROMEDA

The love he has for me engages him
To seek to ruin himself with urgency.
Don't reproach me for this funereal future.
I will pay quite dearly for it.

MEROPE

Let's join our sorrows. The same love binds us.
What does it matter to which of us Perseus offers his
    vows?
The two of us are going to lose him.
His peril reconciles us.

ANDROMEDA and MEROPE

This hero's risking himself for us.
His ruin is certain.
Ah, let him live if it is possible;
Even if he were to live for you.

ANDROMEDA

My love must hide itself and betray itself.
O Heavens! He's going to leave! He's seeking me here-
    abouts.

MEROPE

I intend to spare myself the torture
Of witnessing your farewells.

(Merope leaves)

PERSEUS

(entering) Beautiful Princess, at last, you are allowing
    my presence.

ANDROMEDA

Lord, they ordered me, and I am doing my duty.

PERSEUS

You intend to make me know
That I owe this blessing only to your obedience.
I don't care. Nothing can shake my constancy.
It's been able until this very day to love you without hope..
I'm going to take up your defense with pleasure.
If the only reward I get
Is merely the sweetness of seeing you.

ANDROMEDA

No, don't flatter yourself; I don't wish to hide anything from you.
You love me vainly. Phineas pleased me;
He's been chosen to be my spouse.
Our two hearts are joined—what reward can you hope for,
From so dangerous an enterprise?
Once you become victor, your soul is generous
And you won't wish to break such sweet bonds.

PERSEUS

I will be unhappy, despairing, jealous.
But I shall die happily if you are living happily.

ANDROMEDA

O, Gods!

PERSEUS

Your beautiful eyes are wounded by my glance.
You suffer to see me; my love outrages you.
I am going to seek Medusa, and I love you enough
Not to force you to suffer more.

ANDROMEDA

What! you are leaving me forever!
Perseus, stop, stop!

PERSEUS

What do I hear? O heavens! Beautiful Princess,
What do I see? You are shedding tears?

ANDROMEDA

Ah, from the excess of my sorrows
Know, if possible, the excess of my tenderness.
See to what I'm reduced.
To dampen the ardor which makes you undertake
A battle funereal to your life.
Alas, have I been unable to make myself
Unworthy of your help?
Why aren't you less magnanimous?
Medusa, with a glance, brings certain death.

PERSEUS

You might be her victim.

ANDROMEDA

All the strength of mortals will be useless against her.

PERSEUS

The Son of Jupiter, when love enthuses him
Must go after it with more than human effort.

ANDROMEDA

By the frights of a tender love
Won't you be disarmed?

PERSEUS

I was unaware of your love, and I was going to defend
 you .
Can I be less enthused to help you
Knowing I am loved?

ANDROMEDA

What! You're leaving?

PERSEUS

Love calls me.

ANDROMEDA

You scorn my tears; my cries are superfluous!

PERSEUS

You shall see me fulfill an immortal glory.

ANDROMEDA

Alas! we will never see each other again!

PERSEUS and ANDROMEDA

Ah, your peril is extreme
I see your danger, I don't see mine.
Gods! Save the one I love!
And as for me, myself,
I ask nothing.
Gods! Save the one I love.

(Andromeda leaves)

MERCURY

(emerging from Hell)

Perseus, where are you rushing off to?
What are you going to undertake?

PERSEUS

An unfortunate nation is engaging me to defend it.
I'm running after glory.
If I die, my death will be worthy of being envied.
I leave the care of my life to the God who gave it to me.

MERCURY

That just and powerful God favors your wishes.
And it is through me that he's explaining himself.
He recognizes the generous strength of his blood.
That you are going to attempt with heroic passion
To help the wretched.
But it's not by boldness
That he must hurl your steps into peril.
The assistance of the Gods will be necessary to you.
They are pleased to offer it to you
Do not neglect it.
I am coming to inform all nature
That Jupiter's concerned about your life.
Jealous Juno vainly grumbles about it
And everything. He promises to help you even to Hell.

(Cyclops enter and as they dance give Perseus a sword on behalf of Vulcan, and winged heels similar to those of Mercury.)

ONE CYCLOPS

It's for you, that Vulcan, with his immortal hands
Forged this sword and prepared these wings.
Hasten and display
By a celebrated victory.
Each must go toward Glory,
But a hero must fly to it.

(A troupe of Warrior Nymphs presents a a diamond buckler on behalf of Pallas to Perseus.)

ONE of the Warrior Nymphs

(singing to Perseus as the other nymphs dance)

The most valiant warrior abuses himself
To dare all hope on the strength of his arm.
If you would conquer Medusa
Take this buckler from wise Pallas.
May valor and prudence
When they communicate together
Complete your glorious exploits.
The most furious monster
Vainly resists them.
Peace cannot reign without their assistance.
The universe owes them its happiness.
Nothing can better honor an immortal
Than valor and prudence,
When they communicate together.

(The infernal dignities emerge from Hell and bring Pluto's Helmet with them, which they present to Perseus.)

FEMALE INFERNAL DIGNITY

This helmet is presented to you
In the name of the sovereign emperor of ghosts
For your safety in the midst of peril.
It will spread darkness over you,
Which reigns in our somber dwelling.
This mysterious gift must teach mortals
How one can assure oneself of a favorable success.
Great plans must be hidden
Beneath impenetrable secrecy.

MERCURY, The CHORUSES of CYCLOPS, WARRIOR NYMPHS and INFERNAL DIGNITIES

Let Heaven, Earth and Hell
Let all the universe favor
Your generous undertaking!
Let Heaven, Earth and Hell
Let all the universe favor
The son of the most powerful of Gods!

MERCURY

Your conduct is committed to my care.
Impatience blazes in your eyes.

The glory that is promised to you
Cannot suffer remission.
Follow me, let's leave these parts.

(Mercury and Perseus fly away.)

CHORUSES

Let Heaven, Earth, and Hell,etc..

CURTAIN

ACT III

The Cavern of the Gorgons.

MEDUSA

I've lost the beauty that made me so vain.
I no longer have such beautiful hair
Which in former times, the god of waters
Felt bind his heart in a soft charm.
Pallas, barbarous Pallas,
Was jealous of my attractions
And rendered me more frightful now then once I had
  been beautiful.
But this astonishing excess of deformity
Which her cruelty punishes me with
Will, despite her, reveal
What the excess of my beauty was,
I cannot reveal her cruel vengeance too much.
My head is still proud to have for ornament
Serpents whose hissing
Excites mortal terror.
I bring terror and death everywhere;
Everything changes into rocks at my horrible appear-
  ance

The darts that Jupiter launches from the height of heaven
Have nothing so terrible
As the glance of my eyes.
The greatest gods of heaven, earth and sea
Who care to avenge themselves, rely on me.
If I've lost the sweetness of being the love of the world
I have the new pleasure of becoming its terror.

MEDUSA, EURYALE, and STENONE

O sweet profession for rage
For causing frightful ravages.
Lucky the furor
Which fills the universe—with horror.

(The three Gorgons hear a sweet concert)

In this sad place who can make us hear
The gentle commotion which has just surprised us?
Never mortal with impunity here
Has brought his indiscreet sight.
What concerts! What novelty!
Who can seek the secret horror
Of our fatal retreat?
It's Mercury who's coming into this remote cavern?

(Enter Mercury.)

MEDUSA

My terrible assistance is necessary to you?
Do proud mortals dare displease you?
Do you have to be avenged on them? Must you arm against them
The funereal wrath of my frightful serpents?
Where must my furor fly to?
You have only to name the unfortunate realm
That you want me to desolate.

MERCURY

It's always my dearest wish
To see the whole universe in profound peace.
Don't weary yourself to such a degree in barbarous pleasure
By troubling the repose of the whole world.

MEDUSA

Can I ever cause misfortunes great enough
At the whim of the fury of my distracted heart?
It's from the cruel gods that I learned
To become barbarous.

MERCURY

It's true that a fatal wrath
Has to much blazed against you.
You had but too many charms.

Without Pallas, without her harshness,
You would have troubled hearts
Only with sweet alarms.

MEDUSA

What's the use of discussing with me
Blessings too soon past, which cannot return?
I feel the irreparable loss of it too greatly.
Ah, when one finds oneself frightful
What a cruel memory it is
To think that I was once lovable!

MERCURY

In your misfortune, I can
Only offer you a peaceful sleep.

MEDUSA

With an acute sorrow
Rest is incompatible.

MERCURY

O calm sleep, how charming you are!
What makes you feel a gentle enchantment
Of the saddest solitude.
Your divine power calms uneasiness.
You know how to soften the cruelest torture.
O peaceful sleep, how charming you are!

(to Gorgons)

Let's enjoy rest in this solitary place.

THE THREE GORGONS

No. it's only for rage
That our unhappy hearts are made.
No, rest cannot please us.
We renounce it forever.
No, it's only for rage, etc.

MERCURY

(touching the three Gorgons with his caduces)

You must succumb, you must give yourself up
To the charm that's going to surprise you.

THE THREE GORGONS

We must give up, despite ourselves
To the charm of very sweet sleep.

(The Three Gorgons doze off.)

MERCURY

Perseus, come closer, Medusa is snoozing
Come forward without undue noise, surprise
Such a terrible enemy.
If you dare to look at her, your life is done.

PERSEUS

I will follow the advice you've given me.

MERCURY

I shall leave you in the midst of a formidable peril
I can do nothing more for your life.
Seek your last help
In an unshakable courage.

PERSEUS

A prize which must charm me
Is offered to me by Victory.
What peril can alarm me?
Love and glory
Unite to enthuse me.

(Mercury withdraws. Perseus holding a buckler before his eyes approaches Medusa; he cuts her head off and hides it in a scarf he brought with him.)

PERSEUS

The world's been delivered from a most terrible monster.
Heaven employed my arm.

EURYALE and STENONE (awakened by the sound of his voice and rushing toward where they heard it)

You made Medusa perish! Ah, traitor you will die!
Let him die a horrible death.

(The two Gorgons want to attack Perseus, but the secret virtue of the mask prevents them from seeing him.)

EURYALE and STENONE

But can he make himself invisible?
After her death Medusa still troubles the universe.
It's her blood which produces so many diverse monsters.

(Chrysaor, Pegasus and several other monsters of bizarre and terrible appearance are formed from the blood of Medusa. Chrysaor and Pegasus fly about. Some other monsters also rise up into the air, some rear up, others run, all seek Perseus who is hidden from their sight by the virtue of the power of the helmet. .)

EURYALE and STENONE

Monsters seek your victim.
Avenge the blood which enthuses you.
Serve our furors, arm yourselves
Avenge Medusa, avenge us.

MERCURY

Perseus, go! Fly where love calls you.
Gorgons, henceforth you will be without power.
This place is not dark enough for you.
Come into eternal night.

(Perseus flies, carrying the head of Medusa. The monsters are forced to follow him along, with Euryale and Stenone into Hell into which Mercury forces them to descend.)

EURYALE and STENONE

A profound gulf is opening
And we are falling into Hell.

CURTAIN

ACT IV

An ocean and a shore bordered with rocks.

A TROUPE OF ETHIOPIANS

Let's run, let's all run to admire
The conqueror of Medusa.

PHINEAS

Perseus has returned; everybody is running to honor him.
And the public happiness gives me despair.
No, no, it's time that a vain hope no longer abuses me.

SECOND TROUPE OF ETHIOPIANS

Let's run, let's all run to admire
The conqueror of Medusa.

MEROPE

Let's go sigh in secret.
No, I can no longer show myself
Sad as I am, speechless and confused.

THIRD TROUPE OF ETHIOPIANS

Let's run, let's all run to admire
The conqueror of Medusa.

(The Ethiopians leave.)

PHINEAS

We feel the same sorrows,

Let's flee an unfortunate crowd.

With a common complaint
Let's deplore our common misfortunes.

MEROPE

What chagrins and alarms love has for me
How Perseus has cost my heart displeasures;
His departure, his dangers, made me shed tears.
And his happy return snatched sighs from me.
Perseus has come back, but it's for Andromeda.
For me to offer to his eyes the passion that possesses
  me
Made me vainly rash.
He didn't even deign
To notice my eagerness.
And all the efforts of my extreme passion
Weren't even repaid with a single glance.

PHINEAS

How prodigious heaven is in miracles for Perseus.
What made me think that a furious monster
Would rid me of an odious rival?
Still, despite a thousand obstacles
My rival is victorious.
He's made new paths,
He's flown to hasten his return
And Mercury and Eros
Have taken care, at his wish too lend him wings.
The nation thinks it owes him everything.
You can hear his name echo on the shore.
The King has rushed to honor his courage.
Each, even unto these parts, has come to receive him.
How happy Andromeda seems to see him!
What a triumph for him! What a charming future!
And what rage for me!
And what horrible despair!

PHINEAS and MEROPE

The impetuous winds are slipping their chains
Which forced them to rest.
A sudden storm
Raises the waves.
Vast sea, deep sea
Whose waves are moved by the winds in their wrath
Loving and jealous hearts
Are more agitated than your waves.
Loving and jealous hearts

Are a hundred times more troubled than you.

IDAS and ETHIOPIANS

(entering)

O inexorable Heaven
O deplorable misfortune!

PHINEAS and MEROPE

(aside)

What could cross these very happy lovers?

(to Ethiopians)

What is the cause of these lamentations?

IDAS

Implacable Juno's causing our misfortune.
She's arming the realm of Neptune against us.
A monster must emerge from it who will come to devour
The innocent Andromeda.
And Thetis and her sisters are coming to declare
That hope is no longer permitted,
To see the end of all our ills without this cruel remedy.
Before our eyes The Tritons seized the Princess
And the power of the Gods
Rendered us totally motionless.

They must expose her to a monster on the shores.
To help, Perseus vainly wants to dare all.
His efforts will be useless.
You must give in to Gods, you must give in to Fate
Which is pursuing Andromeda.
Could you imagine seeing such a beautiful life
Ended by a terrible death?

(The Ethiopians place themselves on the rocks which border the shore.)

IDAS and THE ETHIOPIANS

O inexorable fate!
O deplorable misfortune!
Unfortunate princess, alas!
You deserved a more favorable fate.
You didn't deserve
Such a cruel death.
O inexorable fate,
O deplorable misfortune!

PHINEAS

The gods have taken care to avenge us
The pleasure that I feel mixed with pain is hiding itself.

MEROPE

Can you see Andromeda in danger without sorrow?

PHINEAS

Is it from me that death snatches her?
It's for Perseus to be affected.
Love is dying in my heart. Rage will succeed it.
I prefer to see a frightful monster
Devour the ingrate Andromeda
Than see her in the arms of my lucky rival.
Let's wait for her fate to end.
We'll observe the whole thing from a more secluded place.

(Phineas and Merope leave.)

CEPHEUS and CASSIOPIA

Ah! What frightful torture!
Gods! O Gods, what cruelty!

CEPHEUS

Alas, I am losing my daughter! Propitious heaven
Gave her to me for my happiness.
Today, irritated heaven
Intends that a monster ravish her from me.
Heaven, that I've always respected,
Heaven, you who for so long a while kept me alive
Only so as to make me witness this frightful sacrifice?

CEPHEUS and CASSIOPIA

Ah, what terrible torture.
Gods! O Gods what cruelty!

CASSIOPIA

It's my funereal vanity,
It's my crime, great gods, let me be punished for it.
My daughter isn't an accomplice
And your avenging lightning has blazed against her!
Gods! Can you want Andromeda to perish?
Is there nothing in her youth or her beauty
That can bend you?
Does virtue, innocence, deserve
The harshness of your justice?

CEPHEUS and CASSIOPIA

Ah, what frightful torture!
Gods! O Gods, what cruelty!

(The Tritons and Nereides appear in the sea. The Tritons surround Andromeda and attach her to a rock.)

CEPHEUS

Let me expiate such a funereal crime by dying.

CASSIOPIA

From pity, let me obtain a lawful death.

Cruel ones! Don't tie my daughter to a rock.
I'm the one should be tied there.

CEPHEUS, CASSIOPIA, and a CHORUS OF ETHIOPIANS

Divinities of the waves, what wrath inspires you
Against an innocent victim?
She's our only hope; must she be taken from me?
Our prayers, our tears, our cares, can nothing touch you?

ANDROMEDA

Gods! Who've destined me to such a cruel death.
Alas, why'd you flatter me
With the hope of so sweet a destiny?
You, from whom I deserve life, and you, faithful people,
Rejoice in my death with an eternal peace.
I am going to soften the angry gods against us.
And if my mother is criminal
It is I who must calm the celestial wrath
With the blood that I received from her.
Happy to perish for the sake of all,
A charmed memory that I recall, dying,
The attractions, the sweetness of a mutual love
Are the most terrible blows to my fatal destiny.
The Son of Jupiter would have been my spouse.
Ah, how beautiful my life would have been!
Gods! Who've destined me to such a cruel death, etc.

A TRITON

Tremble, proud Queen
Tremble, audacious mortals.
Let your pride learn
How vain is your grandeur.
Tremble, audacious mortals
Beware the wrath of the gods.

CASSIOPIA

Ah, what inhuman vengeance.

CEPHEUS

Andromeda!

CASSIOPIA

My daughter!

ANDROMEDA

O gods!

CASSIOPIA

How cruel the gods, how imperious
In making their hate felt.

CEPHEUS

Andromeda.

CASSIOPIA

My daughter.

ANDROMEDA

O heavens!

(The Monster appears.)

CEPHEUS, and The ETHIOPIANS

The monster's approaching these parts.
Ah, what inhuman vengeance.

THE NEREIDS and The TRITONS

Tremble, audacious mortals, etc.

ANDROMEDA

I don't see Perseus, and I was flattering my pain
With the sad hope of dying before his eyes.

CEPHEUS, CASSIOPIA, and The ETHIOPIANS

See this glorious hero fly!

(Perseus is in the air.)

ANDROMEDA

To risk himself for me; it's vain for him to be so stubborn.

(Perseus flies and battles the monster.)

THE NEREIDES and THE TRITONS

Bold Perseus, stop. Respect
Divine vengeance.

CEPHEUS, CASSIOPIA and THE ETHIOPIANS

Magnanimous hero, fight, carry away victorious,
The prize that belongs to you.

THE NEREIDES and THE TRITONS

The Son of Jupiter braves our wrath.

ALL

The monster's expiring beneath his blows.

A NEREID and A TRITON

Juno has vainly sought our assistance.
We boasted in vain of completing her vengeance.
And Perseus has stronger gods for him than we do.

NEREIDES and TRITONS

Let's go hide beneath the waves.
Our shame must be concealed.
Let's go seek
Profound retreats.
Let's go hide beneath the waves.

(The Sea is appeased; the waves subside and withdraw; the Nereides and Tritons disappear.)

ANDROMEDA, CASSIOPIA, and CEPHEUS

The monster is dead; Perseus is the victor
Perseus is invincible.

(The Ethiopians repeat these verses as Perseus unties Andromeda.)

CEPHEUS and CASSIOPIA

When love enthuses a great heart
It finds nothing impossible.

PERSEUS and ANDROMEDA

Ah! How terrible your danger appeared to me!

ETHIOPIANS

The monster's dead; etc.

(The Ethiopians come down from the rocks, expressing their joy by singing and dancing. Sailors of both sexes mix in with the public rejoicing. One of the Ethiopians sings as the sailors dance.)

ETHIOPIAN

Our hope was shipwrecked.
At last we are enjoying a happy fate.
What happiness to escape the storm
What pleasure to evoke its image,
After we are safe in port.

CEPHEUS

Let's honor forever the glorious hero
Who gives us a happy rest.
His valor makes victory jump at his whim.
The Earth and the waves, each in turn
Are the stage of his glory.
Let's honor forever, etc.

(Andromeda, Cassiopia and The Ethiopians repeat the verses sung by Cepheus, and sailors of both sexes dance, rejoicing for the deliverance of Andromeda.)

AN ETHIOPIAN

What, you do not love?
Unfeeling heart!
What, you don't love?

Nothing is so sweet.
No, don't boast of being invincible.
The gods, the greatest of gods have all loved.

CHORUS

What, you don't love, etc?

AN ETHIOPIAN

Love has no terrible arrows
For a heart that gives in to its blows.

CHORUS

What, you don't love, etc.

AN ETHIOPIAN

For a tender
And faithful lover.
For a lover,
All is charming.
Hope nourishes his flames; its chain is beautiful
It makes its torture a pleasure.

AN ETHIOPIAN

Happy the heart that Love calls!
Unhappy if it delays a moment.

CHORUS

For a lover, etc.

CURTAIN

ACT V

The place prepared for the wedding of Perseus and Andromeda.

MEROPE

O Death! Come end my deplorable fate.
My rival is enjoying too pleasant a destiny.
And I would suffer too much if I weren't to die.
Her happiness renders my life unbearable.
The frightful night of death
Appears less terrifying to me.
O Death! Come and end my deplorable fate.
For fortunate hearts you are horrible
But your horrors have appeal
To a heart that love makes miserable.
O Death! Come end my deplorable fate.

PHINEAS

It's not to tears we must have recourse.
Juno intends that I revenge myself together with her today.
Iris, the faithful interpreter of her will

Is coming by her express command to offer me help.

MEROPE

What can one hope from Juno's help?
Perseus has twice triumphed over her wrath.

PHINEAS

What cannot her wrath
Joined to my jealous distraction do?
Happy is he who can savor a sweet vengeance!
It's the sole hope
Of unlucky lovers.
To serve my furor I've diligently taken arms.
My rival shall not have my treasure as a reward.
If he triumphs over me, it's for a few moments.
Vainly has Andromeda betrayed my constancy.
Love is in vain cahoots with them.
I will smash its charming bonds.
Marriage will deliver to me the ingrate who offends
    me.
She's seen my misery with indifference.
I intend to be unfeeling to her lamentations.
And if I cannot see her heart in my power
I shall enjoy her torments.
Happy is he who can savor a sweet vengeance, etc.
We must distance ourselves from the people who are
    coming forward.
This superb decoration, these rich ornaments
All here increase the violence of my rage.

Let's go hasten the outburst of our grievances.

MEROPE and PHINEAS

Happy is he who can savor a sweet vengeance.

(Merope and Phineas leave.)

(Enter Cepheus, Cassiopia, Perseus, Andromeda, The High Priest of Marriage, his suite, a troupe of courtiers magnificently adorned to be present at the wedding of Perseua and Andromeda.)

HIGH PRIEST

Marriage! O sweet Marriage! Be propitious to our vows!
Come join these faithful lovers,
Come render them happy forever.
Take care to preserve their mutual ardor.
Light, in their favor, the most beautiful of your fires.
May their hearts be filled with eternal sweetness;
May they always be satisfied and always amorous.
Charming marriage, how beautiful are your chains.
When love has forged each bond.
Marriage! O sweet Marriage! Be propitious to our vows!

(As the marriage ceremony is about to begin, it is interrupted by Merope)

MEROPE

Perseus, it's no longer time to keep silent.
I thought to wish you dead,
But my heart is too much in league with you.
And, prepared to avenge myself, I feel a distraction
A hundred times more urgent, and much stronger
Than the urgings of vengeance.
Your rival approaches and he wants your life.
A thousand enemies surround you.
Avoid their furor, employ the help
That the propitious gods are giving you.
Flee, and escape in the midst of the air.
You won't find any other path open.

PERSEUS

Let's arm
we will punish the audacity of rebels.

MEROPE

Save yourself! Profit by my loyal advice.
You must only think of fleeing.

PERSEUS

If the gods have loaned me wings,
It was not to flee danger.

PHINEAS and His Suite

(entering)

Perseus, you must perish
Die and leave Andromeda
To the power of a lucky rival.

CEPHEUS, PERSEUS and Their Suite

Traitors! Receive the fatal punishment
Of the furor that possesses you.

ALL THE COMBATANTS

Give in, give in to our power.
You won't avoid death.

(Perseus, Cepheus and their suite pursue Phineas and his.)

CASSIOPIA and ANDROMEDA

What horrors! What alarms!
Gods! Be moved by my tears!

ALL THE COMBATANTS

Give in, give in to our power, etc.

CEPHEUS

(to Cassiopia) The care of protecting you hereabouts calls me back.
Fear all from a rebellious people.
Whose blood won't they dare to shed?
An arrow, intended for Perseus ,
Struck your sister with a mortal blow.
Juno, implacable towards us
Enthuses the mutineers with her fatal wrath.
Perseus in vain, still fights heatedly.
What's the use of the efforts he's attempting?
Numbers sooner or later overwhelm valor.

PHINEAS and his suite

Don't let him escape; let him perish
This audacious sovereign who pretends to reign hereabouts!

CEPHEUS, CASSIOPIAm and ANDROMEDA

Heaven! O Heaven! Be propitious to us—

PHINEAS and his suite

Don't let him escape; let him perish.

CEPHEUS, CASSIOPIA, and ANDROMEDA

Protect us, O just gods!

PERSEUS

(to those on his side)

Fear nothing. Shut your eyes.
I am going to punish their crime!

(Perseus petrifies Phineas and his suite by revealing to them the head of Medusa.)

PERSEUS

See their funereal punishment!

CEPHEUS, CASSIOPIA, and ANDROMEDA

What a prodigy! What a change!

PERSEUS

The head of Medusa punished them.
Let's cease worrying about cruel fortune.
Heaven is promising us happy days.
Venus is coming to our aid.
She's bringing Eros and Marriage with her.

(The Palace of Venus descends.)

VENUS

Mother, live in peace; your misfortunes are over.
Jupiter is protecting you in favor of his son!

All the gods are pleased to please, this oh- so- powerful god.
And even Juno's wrath, at last is appeased.
Cassiopia, Cepheus, and you, lucky spouses.
Take your place in heaven with us.
Sovereign destinies command
That dazzling fires always surround you.

(Cepheus, Cassiopia, Perseus and Andromeda are elevated to the heavens, and shining stars surround them.)

VENUS, EROS, MARRIAGE, and the CHORUS

Victorious hero, Andromeda is yours!
Your valor and Marriage give her to you.
Glory and Eros are crowning you.
Was there ever so nice a triumph?
Victorious hero, Andromeda is yours.

(The Courtiers of Cepheus, the Ethiopians of both sexes, express their joy by their dancing.)

CURTAIN

ABOUT THE AUTHOR

Frank J. Morlock has written and translated many plays since retiring from the legal profession in 1992. His translations have also appeared on Project Gutenberg, the Alexandre Dumas Père web page, Literature in the Age of Napoléon, Infinite Artistries.com, and Munsey's (formerly Blackmask). In 2006 he received an award from the North American Jules Verne Society for his translations of Verne's plays. He lives and works in México.

www.ingramcontent.com/pod-product-compliance
Lightning Source LLC
LaVergne TN
LVHW041624070426
835507LV00008B/439